Book 1
Python Programming Professional Made Easy

BY SAM KEY

&

Book 2
Facebook Social Power

BY SAM KEY

Book 1
Python Programming Professional Made Easy

By Sam Key

Expert Python Programming Language Success in a Day for Any Computer User!

Programming Box Set #43: Python Programming Professional Made Easy & Facebook Social Power

Table Of Contents

Introduction

I want to thank you and congratulate you for purchasing the book, "Python Programming Professional Made Easy: Expert Python Programming Language Success in a Day for Any Computer User!"

This book contains proven steps and strategies on how to program Python in a few days. The lessons ingrained here will serve as an introduction to the Python language and programming to you. With the little things you will learn here, you will still be able to create big programs.

The book is also designed to prepare you for advanced Python lessons. Make sure that you take note of all the pointers included here since they will help you a lot in the future.

Thanks again for purchasing this book. I hope you enjoy it!

Chapter 1: Introduction to Programming Languages

This short section is dedicated to complete beginners in programming. Knowing all the things included in this chapter will lessen the confusion that you might encounter while learning Python or any programming language.

Computers do not know or cannot do anything by itself. They just appear smart because of the programs installed on them.

Computer, Binary, or Machine Language

You cannot just tell a computer to do something using human language since they can only understand computer language, which is also called machine or binary language. This language only consists of 0's and 1's.

On the other hand, you may not know how to speak or write computer language. Even if you do, it will take you hours before you can tell a computer to do one thing since just one command may consist of hundreds or thousands of 1's and 0's. If you translate one letter in the human alphabet to them, you will get two or three 1's or 0's in return. Just imagine how many 1's and 0's you will need to memorize if you translate a sentence to computer language.

Assembly or Low Level Programming Language

In order to overcome that language barrier, programmers have developed assemblers. Assemblers act as translators between a human and a computer.

However, assemblers cannot comprehend human language. They can only translate binary language to assembly language and vice versa. So, in order to make use of assemblers, programmers need to learn their language, which is also called a low level language.

Unfortunately, assembly language is difficult to learn and memorize. Assembly language consists of words made from mnemonics that only computer experts know. And for one to just make the computer display something to the screen, a programmer needs to type a lot of those words.

High Level Programming Language

Another solution was developed, and that was high level programming languages such as C++, Java, and Python. High level programming languages act as a translator for humans and assembly language or humans to computer language.

Unlike assembly language (or low level language), high level programming languages are easier to understand since they commonly use English words instead of mnemonics. With it, you can also write shorter lines of codes since they already provide commonly used functions that are shortened into one or two keywords.

If you take one command or method in Python and translate it to assembly language, you will have long lines of codes. If you translate it to computer language, you will have thousands of lines composed of 1's and 0's.

In a nutshell, high level programming languages like Python are just translators for humans and computers to understand each other. In order for computers to do something for humans, they need to talk or instruct them via programming languages.

Many high level languages are available today. Among the rest, Python is one of the easiest languages to learn. In the next chapter, you will learn how to speak and write with Python language for your computer to do your bidding.

Chapter 2: Getting Prepped Up

On the previous chapter, you have learned the purpose of programming languages. By choosing this book, you have already decided that Python is the language that you want to use to make your programs. In this chapter, your learning of speaking, writing, and using this language starts.

You, Python, and Your Computer

Before you start writing, take a moment to understand the relationship between you, the programming language, and the computer. Imagine that you are a restaurant manager, and you have hired two foreign guys to cook for the restaurant, which is the program you want to create. The diners in your restaurant are the users of your program.

The first guy is the chef who only knows one language that you do not know. He follows recipes to the letter, and he does not care if the recipe includes him jumping off the cliff. That guy is your computer.

The second guy is the chef's personal translator who will translate the language you speak or write, which is Python, to the language the chef knows. This translator is strict and does not tolerate typos in the recipes he translates. If he finds any mistake, he will tell it right to your face, walk away with the chef, and leave things undone.

He also does not care if the recipe tells the chef to run on circles until he dies. That is how they work. This guy is your programming language.

Since it is a hassle to tell them the recipe while they cook, you decided to write a recipe book instead. That will be your program's code that the translator will read to the chef.

Installing Python

You got two things to get to program in Python. First, get the latest release of Python. Go to this website: https://www.python.org/downloads/.

Download Python 3.4.2 or anything newer than that. Install it. Take note of the directory where you will install Python.

Once you are done with the installation, you must get a source code editor. It is recommended that you get Notepad++. If you already have a source code editor, no need to install Notepad++, too. To download Notepad++, go to: http://www.notepad-plus-plus.org/download/v6.6.9.html. Download and install it.

Version 2.x or 3.x

If you have already visited the Python website to download the program, you might have seen that there are two Python versions that you can download. As of this writing, the first version is Python 3.4.2 and the second version is Python 2.7.8.

About that, it is best that you get the latest version, which is version 3.4.2. The latest version or build will be the only one getting updates and fixes. The 2.7.8 was already declared as the final release for the 2.x build.

Beginners should not worry about it. It is recommended that new Python programmers start with 3.x or later before thinking about exploring the older versions of Python.

Programming and Interactive Mode

Python has two modes. The first one is Programming and the second one is Interactive. You will be using the Interactive mode for the first few chapters of this book. On the other hand, you will be using the Programming mode on the last few chapters.

In Interactive mode, you can play around with Python. You can enter lines of codes on it, and once you press enter, Python will immediately provide a feedback or execute the code you input. To access Python's interactive mode, go to the directory where you installed Python and open the Python application. If you are running on Windows, just open the Run prompt, enter python, and click OK.

In Programming mode, you can test blocks of code in one go. Use a source editor to write the program. Save it as a .py file, and run it as Python program. In Windows, .py files will be automatically associated with Python after you install Python. Due to that, you can just double click the file, and it will run.

Chapter 3: Statements

A program's code is like a recipe book. A book contains chapters, paragraphs, and sentences. On the other hand, a program's code contains modules, functions, and statements. Modules are like chapters that contain the recipes for a full course meal. Procedures or functions are like paragraphs or sections that contain recipes. Statements are like the sentences or steps in a recipe. To code a program with Python, you must learn how to write statements.

Statements

Statements are the building blocks of your program. Each statement in Python contains one instruction that your computer will follow. In comparison to a sentence, statements are like imperative sentences, which are sentences that are used to issue commands or requests. Unlike sentences, Python, or programming languages in general, has a different syntax or structure.

For example, type the statement below on the interpreter:

print("Test")

Press the enter key. The interpreter will move the cursor to the next line and print 'Test' without the single quotes. The command in the sample statement is print. The next part is the details about the command the computer must do. In the example, it is ("test"). If you convert that to English, it is like you are commanding the computer to print the word Test on the program.

Python has many commands and each of them has unique purpose, syntax, and forms. For example, type this and press enter:

1 + 1

Python will return an answer, which is 2. The command there is the operator plus sign. The interpreter understood that you wanted to add the two values and told the computer to send the result of the operation.

Variables

As with any recipe, ingredients should be always present. In programming, there will be times that you would want to save some data in case you want to use them later in your program. And there is when variables come in.

Variables are data containers. They are the containers for your ingredients. You can place almost any type of data on them like numbers or text. You can change the value contained by a variable anytime. And you can use them anytime as long as you need them.

To create one, all you need is to think of a name or identifier for the variable and assign or place a value to it. To create and assign a value to variables, follow the example below:

example1 = 10

On the left is the variable name. On the right is the value you want to assign to the variable. If you just want to create a variable, you can just assign 0 to the variable to act as a placeholder. In the middle is the assignment operator, which is the equal sign. That operator tells the interpreter that you want him to assign a value, which is on its right, to the name or object on the left.

To check if the variable example1 was created and it stored the value 10 in it, type the variable name on the interpreter and press enter. If you done it correctly, the interpreter will reply with the value of the variable. If not, it will reply with a NameError: name <variable_name> is not defined. It means that no variable with that name was created.

Take note, you cannot just create any name for a variable. You need to follow certain rules to avoid receiving syntax errors when creating them. And they are:

- Variable names should start with an underscore or a letter.
- Variable names must only contain letters, numbers, or underscores.
- Variable names can be one letter long or any length.
- Variable names must not be the same with any commands or reserved keywords in Python.
- Variable names are case sensitive. The variable named example1 is different from the variable named Example1.

As a tip, always use meaningful names for your variables. It will help you remember them easily when you are writing long lines of codes. Also, keep them short and use only one style of naming convention. For example, if you create a variable like thisIsAString make sure that you name your second variable like that too: thisIsTheSecondVariable not this_is_the_second_variable.

You can do a lot of things with variables. You can even assign expressions to them. By the way, expressions are combinations of numbers and/or variables together with operators that can be evaluated by the computer. For example:

Example1 = 10

Example2 = 5 + 19

Example3 = Example1 - Example2

If you check the value of those variables in the interpreter, you will get 10 for Example1, 24 for Example2, and -14 for Example3.

Chapter 4: Basic Operators – Part 1

As of this moment, you have already seen three operators: assignment (=), addition (+), and subtraction (-) operators. You can use operators to process and manipulate the data and variables you have – just like how chefs cut, dice, and mix their ingredients.

Types of Python Operators

Multiple types of operators exist in Python. They are:

- **Arithmetic**
- **Assignment**
- **Comparison**
- **Logical**
- **Membership**
- **Identity**
- **Bitwise**

Up to this point, you have witnessed how arithmetic and assignment operators work. During your first few weeks of programming in Python, you will be also using comparison and logical operators aside from arithmetic and assignment operators. You will mostly use membership, identity, and bitwise later when you already advanced your Python programming skills.

As a reference, below is a list of operators under arithmetic and assignment. In the next chapter, comparison and logical will be listed and discussed briefly in preparation for later lessons.

For the examples that the list will use, x will have a value of 13 and y will have a value of 7.

Arithmetic

Arithmetic operators perform mathematical operations on numbers and variables that have numbers stored on them.

> + : **Addition. Adds the values besides the operator.**

z = 13 + 7

z's value is equal to 20.

- : **Subtraction. Subtracts the values besides the operator.**

z = x – y

z's value is equal to 6.

*** : Multiplication. Multiplies the values besides the operator.**

z = x * y

z's value is equal to 91.

/ : Division. Divides the values besides the operator.

z = x / y

z's value is equal to 1.8571428571428572.

**** : Exponent. Applies exponential power to the value to the left (base) with the value to the right (exponent).**

z = x ** y

z's value is equal to 62748517.

// : Floor Division. Divides the values besides the operator and returns a quotient with removed digits after the decimal point.

z = x // y

z's value is equal to 1.

% : Modulus. Divides the values besides the operator and returns the remainder instead of the quotient.

z = x % y

z's value is equal to 6.

Assignment

Aside from the equal sign or simple assignment operator, other assignment operators exist. Mostly, they are combinations of arithmetic operators and the simple assignment operator.

They are used as shorthand methods when reassigning a value to a variable that is also included in the expression that will be assigned to it. Using them in your code simplifies and makes your statements clean.

= : Simple assignment operator. It assigns the value of the expression on its right hand side to the variable to its left hand side.

z = x + y * x – y % x

z's value is equal to 97.

The following assignment operators work like this: it applies the operation first on the value of the variable on its left and the result of the expression on its right. After that, it assigns the result of the operation to the variable on its left.

+= : Add and Assign

x += y

x's value is equal to 20. It is equivalent to x = x + y.

-= : Subtract and Assign

x −= y

x's value is equal to 6. It is equivalent to x = x – y.

*= : Multiply and assign

x *= y

x's value is equal to 91. It is equivalent to x = x * y.

/= : Divide and assign

x /= y

x's value is equal to 1.8571428571428572. It is equivalent to x = x / y.

**= : Exponent and Assign

x **= y

x's value is equal to 62748517. It is equivalent to x = x ** y.

//= : Floor Division and Assign

x //= y

x's value is equal to 1. It is equivalent to x = x // y.

%= : Modulus and Assign

x %= y

x's value is equal to 6. It is equivalent to x = x % y.

Multiple Usage of Some Operators

Also, some operators may behave differently depending on how you use them or what values you use together with them. For example:

z = “sample” + “statement”

As you can see, the statement tried to add two strings. In other programming languages, that kind of statement will return an error since their (+) operator is dedicated for addition of numbers only. In Python, it will perform string concatenation that will append the second string to the first. Hence, the value of variable z will become “samplestatement”.

On the other hand, you can use the (-) subtraction operator as unary operators. To denote that a variable or number is negative, you can place the subtraction operator before it. For example:

z = 1 - -1

The result will be 2 since 1 minus negative 1 is 2.

The addition operator acts as a unary operator for other languages; however, it behaves differently in Python. In some language, an expression like this: +(-1), will be treated as positive 1. In Python, it will be treated as +1(-1), and if you evaluate that, you will still get negative 1.

To perform a unary positive, you can do this instead:

--1

In that example, Python will read it as –(-1) or -1 * -1 and it will return a positive 1.

Chapter 5: Basic Operators – Part 2

Operators seem to be such a big topic, right? You will be working with them all the time when programming in Python. Once you master or just memorize them all, your overall programming skills will improve since most programming languages have operators that work just like the ones in Python.

And just like a restaurant manager, you would not want to let your chef serve food with only unprocessed ingredients all the time. Not everybody wants salads for their dinner.

Comparison

Aside from performing arithmetic operations and storing values to variables, Python can also allow you to let the computer compare expressions. For example, you can ask your computer if 10 is greater than 20. Since 10 is greater than 20, it will reply with True – meaning the statement you said was correct. If you have compared 20 is greater than 10 instead, it will return a reply that says False.

== : Is Equal

z = x == y

z's value is equal to FALSE.

!= : Is Not Equal

z = x != y

z's value is equal to True.

> : Is Greater Than

z = x > y

z's value is equal to True.

< : Is Less Than

z = x < y

z's value is equal to FALSE.

>= : Is Greater Than or Equal

z = x >= y

z's value is equal to True.

<= : Is Less Than or Equal

z = x <= y

z's value is equal to FALSE.

Note that the last two operators are unlike the combined arithmetic and simple assignment operator.

Logical

Aside from arithmetic and comparison operations, the computer is capable of logical operations, too. Even simple circuitry can do that, but that is another story to tell.

Anyway, do you remember your logic class where your professor talked about truth tables, premises, and propositions? Your computer can understand all of that. Below are the operators you can use to perform logic in Python. In the examples in the list, a is equal to True and b is equal to False.

and : Logical Conjunction AND. It will return only True both the propositions or variable besides it is True. It will return False if any or both the propositions are False.

w = a and a

x = a and b

y = b and a

z = b and b

w is equal to True, x is equal to False, y is equal to False, and z is equal to False.

or : Logical Disjunction OR. It will return True if any or both of the proposition or variable beside it is True. It will return False if both the propositions are False.

w = a or a

x = a or b

y = b or a

z = b or b

w is equal to True, x is equal to True, y is equal to True, and z is equal to False.

not : Logical Negation NOT. Any Truth value besides it will be negated. If True is negated, the computer will reply with a False. If False is negated, the computer will reply with a True.

w = not a

x = not b

w is equal to False and x is equal to True.

If you want to perform Logical NAND, you can use Logic Negation NOT and Logical Conjunction AND. For example:

w = not (a and a)

x = not (a and b)

y = not (b and a)

z = not (b and b)

w is equal to False, x is equal to True, y is equal to True, and z is equal to True.

If you want to perform Logical NOR, you can use Logic Negation NOT and Logical Disjunction OR. For example:

w = not (a or a)

x = not (a or b)

y = not (b or a)

z = not (b or b)

w is equal to False, x is equal to False, y is equal to False, and z is equal to True.

You can perform other logical operations that do not have Python operators by using conditional statements, which will be discussed later in this book.

Order of Precedence

In case that your statement contains multiple types or instances of operators, Python will evaluate it according to precedence of the operators, which is similar to the PEMDAS rule in Mathematics. It will evaluate the operators with the highest precedence to the lowest. For example:

z = 2 + 10 / 10

Instead of adding 2 and 10 first then dividing the sum by 10, Python will divide 10 by 10 first then add 2 to the quotient instead since division has a higher precedence than subtraction. So, instead of getting 1.2, you will get 3.0. In case that it confuses you, imagine that Python secretly adds parentheses to the expression. The sample above is the same as:

z = 2 + (10 / 10)

If two operators with the same level of precedence exist in one statement, Python will evaluate the first operator that appears from the left. For example:

z = 10 / 10 * 2

The value of variable z will be 2.

Take note that any expressions inside parentheses or nested deeper in parentheses will have higher precedence than those expressions outside the parentheses. For example:

z = 2 / ((1 + 1) * (2 – 4))

Even though the division operator came first and has higher precedence than addition and subtraction, Python evaluated the ones inside the parentheses first and evaluated the division operation last. So, it added 1 and 1, subtracted 4 from 2, multiplied the sum and difference of the two previous operations, and then divided the product from 2. The value of variable z became -0.5.

Below is a reference for the precedence of the operations. The list is sorted from operations with high precedence to operators with low precedence.

- **Exponents**
- **Unary**
- **Multiplication, Division, Modulo, and Floor Division**
- **Addition, and Subtraction**
- **Bitwise**
- **Comparison**
- **Assignment**
- **Identity**
- **Membership**
- **Logical**

Truth Values

The values True and False are called truth values – or sometimes called Boolean data values. The value True is equal to 1 and the value False is equal to 0. That means that you can treat or use 1 as the truth value True and 0 as the truth value False. Try comparing those two values in your interpreter. Code the following:

True == 1

False == 0

The interpreter will return a value of True – meaning, you can interchange them in case a situation arises. However, it is advisable that that you use them like that sparingly.

Another thing you should remember is that the value True and False are case sensitive. True != TRUE or False != false. Aside from that, True and False are Python keywords. You cannot create variables named after them.

You might be wondering about the use of truth values in programming. The answer is, you can use them to control your programs using conditional or flow control tools. With them, you can make your program execute statements when a certain condition arises. And that will be discussed on the next chapter.

Chapter 6: Functions, Flow Control, and User Input

With statements, you have learned to tell instructions to the computer using Pythons. As of now, all you know is how to assign variables and manipulate expressions. And the only command you know is print. Do you think you can make a decent program with those alone? Maybe, but you do not need to rack your brains thinking of one.

In this chapter, you will learn about functions and flow control. This time, you will need to leave the interpreter or Interactive mode. Open your source code editor since you will be programming blocks of codes during this section.

Functions

Statements are like sentences in a book or steps in a recipe. On the other hand, functions are like paragraphs or a recipe in a recipe book. Functions are blocks of code with multiple statements that will perform a specific goal or goals when executed. Below is an example:

```
def recipe1():

        print("Fried Fish Recipe")

        print("Ingredients:")

        print("Fish")

        print("Salt")

        print("Steps:")

        print("1. Rub salt on fish.")

        print("2. Fry fish.")

        print("3. Serve.")
```

The function's purpose is to print the recipe for Fried Fish. To create a function, you will need to type the keyword def (for define) then the name of the function. In the example, the name of the function is recipe1. The parentheses are important to be present there. It has its purpose, but for now, leave it alone.

After the parentheses, a colon was placed. The colon signifies that a code block will be under the function.

To include statements inside that code block, you must indent it. In the example, one indentation or tab was used. To prevent encountering errors, make sure that all the statements are aligned and have the same number of indentations.

To end the code block for the function, all you need is to type a statement that has the same indentation level of the function declaration.

By the way, all the statements inside a function code block will not be executed until the function is called or invoked. To invoke the function, all you need is to call it using its name. To invoke the function recipe1, type this:

```
recipe1()
```

And that is how simple functions work.

Flow Control

It is sad that only one recipe can be displayed by the sample function. It would be great if your program can display more recipes. And letting the user choose the recipe that they want to be displayed on the program would be cool. But how can you do that?

You can do that by using flow control tools in Python. With them, you can direct your program to do something if certain conditions are met. In the case of the recipe listing program, you can apply flow control and let them see the recipes by requesting it.

If Statement

The simplest control flow tool you can use for this type of project is the if statement. Have you been wondering about truth values? Now, you can use them with if statements.

An *if statement* is like a program roadblock. If the current condition of your program satisfies its requirements, then it will let it access the block of statements within it. It is like a function with no names, and instead of being invoked to work, it needs you to satisfy the conditions set to it. For example:

```
a = 2

if a == 2:

        print(“You satisfied the condition!”)

        print(“This is another statement that will be executed!”)

if a == (1 + 1):

        print(“You satisfied the condition again!”)

        print(“I will display the recipe for Fried Fish!”)

        recipe1()
```

If you will translate the first if statement in English, it will mean that: if variable a is equals to 2, then print the sentence inside the parentheses. Another way to translate it is: if the comparison between variable a and the number 2 returns True, then print the sentence inside the parentheses.

As you can see, the colon is there and the statements below the if statement are indented, too. It really is like a function.

User Input

You can now control the flow of your program and create functions. Now, about the recipe program, how can the user choose the recipe he wants to view? That can be done by using the input() command. You can use it like this:

a = input("Type your choice here and press enter: ")

Once Python executes that line, it will stop executing statements. And provide a prompt that says "Type your choice here: ". During that moment, the user will be given a chance to type something in the program. If the user press enter, Python will store and assign the characters the user typed on the program to variable a. Once that process is done, Python will resume executing the statements after the input statement.

In some cases, programmers use the input command to pause the program and wait for the user to press enter. You can do that by just placing input() on a line.

With that, you can make a program that can capture user input and can change its flow whenever it gets the right values from the user. You can create a recipe program that allows users to choose the recipe they want. Here is the code. Analyze it. And use the things you have learned to improve it. Good luck.

```
print("Enter the number of the recipe you want to read.")

print("1 - Fried Fish")

print("2 - Fried Egg")

print("Enter any character to Exit")

choice = input("Type a Number and Press Enter: ")


if choice == "1":

        print("Fried Fish Recipe")

        print("Ingredients:")

        print("Fish")
```

```
    print("Salt")
    print("Steps:")
    print("1. Rub salt on fish.")
    print("2. Fry fish.")
    print("3. Serve.")
    pause = input("Press enter when you are done reading.")

if choice == "2":
    print("Fried Egg Recipe")
    print("Ingredients:")
    print("Egg")
    print("Salt")
    print("Steps:")
    print("1. Fry egg.")
    print("2. Sprinkle Salt.")
    print("3. Serve.")
    pause = input("Press enter when you are done reading.")
```

Conclusion

Thank you again for purchasing this book!

I hope this book was able to help you to learn the basics of Python programming.

The next step is to learn more about Python! You should have expected that coming.

Kidding aside, with the current knowledge you have in Python programming, you can make any programs like that with ease. But of course, there are still lots of things you need to learn about the language such as loops, classes, and etcetera.

Finally, if you enjoyed this book, please take the time to share your thoughts and post a review on Amazon. We do our best to reach out to readers and provide the best value we can. Your positive review will help us achieve that. It'd be greatly appreciated!

Thank you and good luck!

Book 2
Facebook Social Power

By Sam Key

The Most Powerful Represented Facebook Guide to Making Money on anything on the Planet!

Programming Box Set #43: Python Programming Professional Made Easy & Facebook Social Power

Table Of Contents

Introduction

I want to thank you and congratulate you for purchasing the book, "Learning the Social Power of Facebook: The Most Powerful Represented Facebook Guide to Making Money on anything on the Planet!"

This book contains proven steps and strategies on how to learn ways to use Facebook as a means to generate money for whatever business you have.

As you well may know by now, Facebook can be an amazing tool to promote your business, and of course, make money from it. However, not everyone knows how to do it, but with the help of this book, you'll learn everything you need to know about how to use Facebook to attract people's attention, and be successful in the world of business.

What are you waiting for? Start reading this book now and make money through Facebook as soon as possible!

Thanks again for purchasing this book, I hope you enjoy it!

Chapter 1: Make Use of Advertising based on E-Commerce

Because of Facebook's Ad Platform, a lot of marketers have been able to reach a wide range of audience because they get to put ads on their Facebook Pages that takes those who click the links to E-Commerce sites, so just the fact that these people get to see their pages already add a lot of traffic to their sites, and may allow people to get paid.

Oftentimes, people overlook the ads-to-direct sites but knowing how to go forth with it is very beneficial because it has a three-way approach that will help you earn a lot of money. Basically, this approach goes as follows:

FB Ads—Discount Pages/Website Sales—Buyers/Customers

One example of a company that benefited a lot from E-Commerce based Advertising through Facebook is Vamplets.com. Vamplets.com is popular for selling plush dolls—but these dolls aren't just regular plush dolls, as they are Vampire Plushies. When Vamplets used this kind of advertising, they were able to achieve 300% ROI, which is definitely a mean feat.

So, how then are you going to be able to use E-Commerce based Advertising for your business? Follow the pointers below and you'll understand how.

Choose your Audience

First and foremost, you have to choose your target demographic so that sales funnel will be easier to be filled. Facebook will allow you to choose between one of the following:

- Custom Audience from Your Website
- Custom Audience from MailChimp
- Data File Custom Audience
- Custom Audience from Your Mobile App

Once you're able to choose your target demographic, it will be easy for you to convert an ad to money because these people will be interested in what you have to offer because you're no longer going to be generalizing things.

You can also choose your audience via the Facebook Audience Insights Category. Here, you'll be able to find people who are interested in your campaign, based on pages that they have liked, so that you'd know that they would like to see what your business is all about. This is called interest-based campaigning.

You can also try using Lookalike Audiences. You can do this by making use of your existing audience, and then pick the next group of people who act and feel similar to your original audience so your posts would be able to reach more people, and you'd get more traffic and revenue, as well. It would be nice to test audiences, too, so you'd know who's interested in your services.

For example, you're selling clothes for pregnant women. You really cannot expect people who are single or who are still in High School click your ads, or like your page, because of course, they're not in that stage of their lives yet. So, make sure that you choose audiences that you know will listen to what you have to say.

Then, go on and place a Facebook Pixel to the footer of your page, and your ads will then be connected to Facebook. You can also choose to send traffic to one audience group this week, then to another group the next.

Make Proper Segments for Visitors of Your Homepage

Of course, you have to make sure that your homepage gets the attention of many because if it doesn't, and if people feel alienated by it, you also cannot expect that you'll gain profit from it. The three basic things that you have to have in your homepage include:

- New Sales Items
- Branding Ads
- Other Promotional Ads

Make Segments for Categories and Products

You can also place ads in various categories of your website so that even if your customer does not check out all the items he placed in the cart, your website will still gain some revenue because more often than not, customers like to buy products based on ads that were able to get through to them.

Chapter 2: Use Fan Marketing E-Commerce

Basically, Fan Marketing E-Commerce is the means of promoting your business by making sure that you post ads through your page and have those ads appear on the newsfeeds of your target demographic.

Research has it that fans become more interested in a new product or business when they see ads, instead of when they learn about the said products through contests or just from other people. Why? Simply because ads are more professional ways of getting people's attention and marketing products, and Facebook definitely makes that easy.

However, it's not enough that you just have a fanpage. You have to make sure that you actually use the said page and that it doesn't get stuck. You can do this by making sure that you constantly post a thing or two, and that you interact with your fans, as well.

You see, a study held in 2011 showed that although over a hundred thousand people may like a certain page, sometimes, revenue only gets up by 7%, because the owners of the fan pages do not interact with their fans and have not posted anything in a while. You also have to make sure that you stay relevant by being able to attract new fans from time to time.

Once you do this right, you'll be able to create the process of:

FB Ads—FB Fans—See Posts—Click to Website—Buyers/Customers

Some of those who have greatly benefited from Fan Marketing Strategies include:

- Baseball Roses, a company that sells artificial roses made from old baseball balls, who gained over 437% of ROI with the help of Facebook Fan Marketing;
- Superherostuff.com, a website that sells merchandise based on famous superheroes, such as t-shirts, jackets, hoodies, shoes, and more, gained over 150% ROI, and;
- Rosehall Kennel Breeds, a company that specializes in selling German Shepherds, gained over a whopping 4,000% of ROI for its fan acquisition speed alone—and that's definitely something that should inspire you.

So, what exactly did these companies do and how did they make use of Facebook Fan Marketing E-Commerce for their own benefit? Here are some tips that you can follow:

1. **Make sure that you post a new update after your last update is gone from people's newsfeeds.** Sometimes, you see posts in your feed for even a day or two after posting, but there are also times when they are

gone after just a couple of minutes or hours. It actually varies due to how fans see or react on those posts and Facebook's EdgeRank Algorithm will be able to give you a glimpse of how your post is doing, based on three main factors, which are:

a. **Likes per Post.** You'd know that people are interested in your posts when they actually make it a point to like the said posts, and it's great because likes are always updated in real time, and will also let your posts stay longer on people's newsfeeds. Therefore, make sure to check the numbers of likes regularly.

b. **Comments per Post.** Comments are always time-stamped, but you cannot always rely on these as not everyone like to comment on posts, and you cannot define whether the posts appear on people's feeds, or they're simply too lazy to comment.

c. **Impressions per Post.** This is basically the number of times a single status has been viewed. While the numbers update as more and more people get to see your post, there are also times when the number stay stagnant only because Facebook refuses to update, so may have to wait a while to see the real numbers.

A good way of trying to gauge your influence on Facebook is by posting an hourly status, then make sure that you record the number of likes, comments, and impressions, and then record the data on Excel. Make a graph, then see the ratio of how much your posts appear on one's feeds, and decide the average number of posts that you have to do per day or per week.

2. **Make sure that the things you post are not redundant.** People these days have really short attention span so it would be nice if you know how to post varied content. Make sure that your fans have something to come back to each day, and that they don't get bored with whatever it is that you have on your website and won't click the "dislike" button.

3. **Do some marketing.** Again, you're trying to make money by means of promoting your products so you have to do a lot of marketing via Facebook. An easy way of doing this is by giving your fans discount codes that they can use if they're interested in buying your products so that they'd constantly check your page.

4. **Make sure that social sharing buttons are open.** While you may use Facebook as the original platform for advertising your services, you also have to realize that it's important to share your content on other websites or social networking sites so that more people would get to see what you have to offer. Also, make sure that your page is set to public because you really cannot expect people to know what you want them to know if your page is set to private. When your page is public, they'll be able to like, comment, and share your posts, which will bring you more traffic and

more revenue. Then, connect your Facebook Page to your other social media accounts so that whenever you post updates on your Facebook Page, the updates will be sent to all your other accounts, as well.

5. **Don't ever try hard-selling tactics.** It's always better to be subtle because people hate it when they feel like their feeds are full of pages that just sell their products outright without making the fans understand what they're all about. So, try asking your fans some questions, or create polls about what kind of products or services they like but never just put up ads or ask them to "buy your products" right away without helping them know that you're their "friend" and that you want them to know what's best in the market right now. You can also place behind the scenes videos of what goes on in your company, or post testimonials from past customers to get the curiosity of your fans running. This way, you get to be trustworthy and your business will be more authoritative, and people would be more interested.
6. **And, make sure that you provide good customer service.** For a Facebook Page to be successful, it doesn't have to be bombarded with ads, you also have to make sure that you get to be friends with your customers and that loyalty and trust are built. For example, when one of your fans posts questions or queries on your page, take time to answer the said questions, and make sure that you reply as soon as possible so that you get to create some sense of urgency and that people will know that you're there.

Keep these tips in mind and you'll surely be able to make use of your Facebook Page to give you a lot of profit. Oh, and make sure to have ample amounts of patience, too!

Chapter 3: Connect Facebook Ads to E-Mail

Another way of making use of Facebook to gain revenue is by connecting ads to e-mails. Basically, it's a way of promoting content to your e-mail subscribers so that it will be easier for your fans to know about your new products or services, or to know if there are contests or events coming up based on the updates that you have sent.

Basically, when Facebook ads are sent to people's e-mails, there are more chances of acquiring a larger number of future subscribers. And Facebook makes this easy for you as they have a feature that allows you to add E-mail lists to your Fan Page so that whenever you post an update, your e-mail list will automatically get to know it, too.

The target formula is as follows:

FB Ad—Squeeze—E-mail Sign Up—E-mail Open—E-mail Click to Visit—Buyers/Customers

So, in order for you to be successful in this kind of marketing tactic, you first have to get a target demographic of e-mail subscribers. While it may be easy to just post an invite so your fans would want to be part of your e-mail list, it will be nice to filter people who probably won't open your e-mails and choose people who would be interested in what you have to offer. You can do this by adding information to the Facebook Ad Copy Page. The information that you need are as follows:

- Gender
- Age
- Location
- Interests
- Relationship Status
- Educational Attainment/Level
- Workplace
- Pages that have been liked (So you'd get to see if they would like the posts that you'd be making)

Then, go on and upload the e-mail list on your Facebook Page by giving Facebook a list of e-mails from MailChimp or any other AutoResponder Service, so that the e-mail addresses of your fans will be synchronized to your page.

Effective Message Integration

It's so easy to send a message but it's never really easy to make sure that those messages are effective. However, there are a couple of tips that you can keep in mind:

- Optimize Facebook Ad Headlines with Catchy Subject Lines so that your fans will be interested to open your e-mails. Examples include:
    - Do Gamers dream of DOTA II?
    - Why your 12 year old likes Miley Cyrus
    - 8 Most Annoying Social Media Moments of 2014
    - 3 Ways to Improve Your Life

  Basically, you have to make sure that your subject lines have a lot to do with your content and with your line of business so that your fans won't be confused and they'd be interested in what you have to say.
- Add your fans' testimonials and comments about your services so others would know that you are for real.
- Add images into your e-mails. After all, people have short attention span and they would appreciate it if they get to see images as part of your e-mails because these would get their attention more and would help them picture what you are talking about.
- Let your fans know that you are going to send another e-mail blast by updating your Facebook status.
- Tease some of the contents of your e-mail on your status updates so that your fans will be hyped up and will be curious to open their e-mails.
- Make use of Facebook Landing Tabs, and Social Log-in Software, so that whenever your fans open their e-mails, it will automatically add traffic to your Facebook Page, and your website, as well.
- Put some sort of disclaimer, or a line that allows your fans to unsubscribe if they want to, because they have to know that you're not actually forcing them to read your messages and that they have the choice to unsubscribe from your list.
- And don't forget to send Thank You messages. If you want to foster a great relationship with your fans, you have to let them know that you're thankful

that they're around, and that they're part of your list, so that they will realize that it's substantial to read the content that you are sending, and that it's important to be a fan of yours, instead of just talking about yourself all the time, without thinking of your fans. After all, without them, you won't gain any profit so you have to be grateful that they're around.

You can also run Geo-targeted ads, or ads that are meant for people who live in one location alone, so that the e-mails would feel more personal and so that your fans will know that you are really thinking of them. Sometimes, targeting people who are in the same vicinity as you is more effective because you get to really connect with them as you experience the same things and you'd know that they are more likely to try your products, unlike those that live in far away places.

If you're able to be successful with Facebook E-mail marketing, you can definitely gain more traffic and more revenue. One of those Fortune 500 Companies actually gained 400% ROI just because of its e-mail subscribers, so you can expect that you'll gain more, too, but only if you follow the tips given above. Good Luck!

Chapter 4: Making Use of Your Ad-Supported Sites

Ad-Supported sites are those that run advertisements and allow the said ads to be shared to your Facebook Page.

This is especially helpful for those whose businesses are really situated online, and those whose blogs or websites are their bread and butter. So, if that's the case, it would be important to create a Facebook Page that's connected to your blog or your website so that things would be formalized more. People like it when they see that a certain website has a Facebook Page because they feel like they'd get to be updated more without having to go to the website.

The formula for this is as follows:

FB Ad—FB Fan—See Post—Click to Website—Click Ad

So basically, when people click ads on your website that take them to your Facebook Page and Vice Versa, you not only gain traffic, you get to be paid, as well. This is similar as the popular Pay-Per-Click Advertising tactic. And also, when you get more fans from various parts of the world, your revenue will increase even more mainly because your content now gets to reach a large number of people, which evidently is beneficial for your business.

Proud Single Moms, a site targeted to help single mothers, gained over $5,000 for Facebook Ads alone that were promoted on their Facebook Page that has around 100,000 fans. On their blog, they made sure that they posted topics that single mothers would be able to relate to, and they also made sure that they used keywords that would give them high search rank on search engines such as Google, or Yahoo.

You can make use of Keyword Tools that are found online to find the perfect keywords that are related to your niche. Once you use these keywords in your posts, you'll be able to generate traffic and revenue.

The main reason why ads on Facebook are so effective is the fact that almost everyone in the world has a Facebook account, so of course, you can expect them to see your posts and the ads that are on your page, too. Plus, when you post links of your blog's content to your Facebook Page, there are more chances that people will get to read these posts because of course, they found it on Facebook, and they didn't use the web just so they could see your website. And these days, that is very important. The key is to be reachable.

Proud Single Moms made sure that they posted the links of blog post updates each day and in just a matter of six months, they were able to create another website that gave them more revenue.

Chapter 5: Other Tips

Aside from the techniques given above, you can also make use of these Facebook Marketing tactics to make sure that your business gains more profit:

Ads through SMS

While it may not be as popular as other Facebook Marketing tips, the combination of Facebook Ads and Text Messaging have slowly been gaining the attention of many for being a fast-paced approach when it comes to advertising products and services. In fact, around 24% of marketers on mobile have gained more ROI just because people have responded to text messages regarding product promotions, and have tried the coupons that they gave away through text, too.

This is especially effective for those with business that are related to food as free coupons that were sent to Facebook fans helped these fans to be more interested to try certain products that were being sold, and have visited the restaurants more often in hopes that they'd be given more information and more freebies, too. When people feel like they know the latest news about a certain establishment or a certain product, it's easy for them to appreciate the said establishment and so they get to patronize it more. This then gave the restaurants around $60,000 more revenue, which is definitely something good!

Give Some Offers that they won't be able to refuse!

Mostly everyone want freebies, because money is really hard to come by these days and not everything is affordable, so of course, they feel like it's nice to be able to get some goodies or services for free. Facebook Offers actually help you create deals with your fans that are not available on other social media platforms.

Basically, you ask your customers to like your page and leave their e-mail addresses so that you can send them coupons or offers that they can redeem in your store. First, make the offers exclusive to your fans then when it gets successful, you can then make more offers for people outside your circle so that more people would be excited to try your products and see what you have to offer.

Don't think about losing profit. More often than not, when you give things away for free, people will be more interested to try your other products and so of course, they'd be paying you in the future, so it's like you have made them your investment and soon enough, you'll benefit from them.

Create Apps for them

A lot of people these days rely on apps that they could use to open certain websites or pages, and of course, if you create an app for your business, it will be easy for them to read your content and it will be easy for you to reach them. They wouldn't have to deal with the hassle of using the browser just so they could see some offers or read articles connected to a certain topic that they would like to learn about. Also, it's better if you add links to your Facebook Page to the app that you have created so that everything will be merged together.

You can also create Facebook Ads without creating a Facebook Page

You can do this by selecting the Clicks to Website option of Facebook or the Website Conversions tab. People will still get to see your ads on the right side of their pages. You know, those ads that appear near the chat sidebar, so in a way, you still get to promote your business, but having Facebook Pages are still way better because then the ads appear on the main feeds and not just on the right side tabs.

Create a catchy headline

Just like how important it is to create effective e-mail subject lines, it's also important to create catchy ad headlines because these will attract people's attention and will allow people to understand what you and your business are all about.

The rule of thumb is to make sure that the headline of your ad is the same as the title of your page so it will be easily recognizable. It would also be helpful if you pair it up with an image that you have created so that people will be able to connect the said image to your business and it will be easy for them to remember your ad.

Make use of Sponsored Stories, too

You see, sponsored stories are the results of how people interact on your page or how they appreciate your content. Basically, whenever someone likes your posts or updates, or when they comment on or share your content, it creates "Facebook Stories". To make sure that these stories appear on a lot of people's newsfeeds, you have to pay a minimal fee, so it's like you get to easily advertise your content and you make sure that people actually get to see them.

But make sure that you choose the best bidding and advertising options

What's good about Facebook is that it allows you to choose the best kind of bidding option that will be good for your business. For example, you can choose whether you want to gain revenue through clicks, or through impressions then you can then reach your objective after you have customized your bids.

You can also choose whether you'd like to pay for your content to be advertised by paying daily, or by paying for a lifetime. The advantages of paying for a lifetime is that you'd know that your content will always be published and that you'd basically have nothing else to worry about, but the thing is that when you want to change the products you are advertising or if you're going to close your business down, it's like you'll get people confused because they'll still see ads from your old site, and they'd keep looking for your services. So, it's recommended that you just pay for the ads daily or on a case to case basis, say there's an event that's coming up and the like, so that it won't be hard for you to reach your followers and gain potential fans in the process, too.

When making use of image ads, make sure that text is only 20%

You would not want to bombard your followers with too many texts and images in just one post. Plus, your image ads won't be approved if they contain more than 20% of text.

In order to know if your ads are following Facebook's guidelines, check out the Facebook Grid Tool that will help you see how your ad looks and what needs to be changed, if necessary.

Let others help you

Sometimes, two heads are better than one, and it's great because when you add another admin to your page, they can also update your page so whenever you're busy or if you cannot answer queries right away, these other admins can help you out.

Just make sure that you choose admins that you can trust and that they know a lot about your business so the things they will be posting will be substantial, too. To do this, just go to the Ad Manager option of Facebook, then click Ad Account Roles, and choose Add a User. Make sure that the person you will add as an admin is your friend on Facebook and that his e-mail address can easily be searched through Facebook, too.

And, don't forget to choose the revenue model that is right for you

To do this, you may have to try each technique first, but don't worry because sooner or later, you'll find the one that proves to be the most effective for your business.

In the marketing business, trial and error really is one of the biggest keys to success, so don't worry if you feel like you aren't being successful right away. Take chances and soon enough, you'll be on the path to success. Good Luck!

Conclusion

Thank you again for purchasing this book!

I hope this book was able to help you understand how you can use Facebook to advertise your business and gain lots of revenue.

The next step is to follow the techniques listed here, and don't be afraid to try each one because sooner or later, you'll find the perfect fit for you. Advertise through Facebook and let your business soar!

Thank you and good luck!

Check Out My Other Books

Below you'll find some of my other popular books that are popular on Amazon and Kindle as well. Simply click on the links below to check them out. Alternatively, you can visit my author page on Amazon to see other work done by me.

Android Programming in a Day

Python Programming in a Day

C Programming Success in a Day

C Programming Professional Made Easy

JavaScript Programming Made Easy

PHP Programming Professional Made Easy

C ++ Programming Success in a Day

Windows 8 Tips for Beginners

HTML Professional Programming Made Easy

If the links do not work, for whatever reason, you can simply search for these titles on the Amazon website to find them.

www.ingramcontent.com/pod-product-compliance
Lightning Source LLC
Chambersburg PA
CBHW060932050326
40689CB00013B/3062
* 9 7 8 1 5 1 1 7 9 4 2 2 0 *